OPTIONS TRADING

BLUEPRINT TO MAKING MONEY WITH OPTIONS TRADING, INDEX OPTIONS, BINARY OPTIONS AND STOCK OPTIONS

BY: DANIEL MITCHELL

Free Bonus: Join Our Book Club and Receive Free Gifts Instantly

Click Below For Your Bonus:
https://success321.leadpages.co/freebodymindsoul/

TABLE OF CONTENTS

INTRODUCTION

The world of finance has competing reputations. On the one hand, there is the prestige and power that goes hand-in-hand with investment banking and so-called high finance. Not only is money made, but connections to the elite are nurtured, huge amounts of capital coalesce, and the livelihoods of tens of thousands of workers are on the line. Think mergers and acquisitions, where multi-billion-dollar companies work with each other, shedding thousands of jobs in a deal or building new factories and development poverty-stricken rural areas into gleaming new towns.

On the positive side, take a new rural development for an example. An oilfield in Midwest America cannot be developed without large investment, and often the banks are the only ones who can provide enough money to start the project. The money pours into the rural area, and suddenly there is a boom and everyone is happy. The bankers are who made it all happen.

On the other hand, finance is viewed with contempt from a large segment of the population. The bankers are those filthy Wall Streeters who do not care about Main Street – all they want is to milk every penny out of Joe down the block. When Joe loses his job at the oilfield due to a merger decided 2000 miles away, another banking institution, equally far away, yet cozily connected to the first company, takes his house. The financiers live in 50th-floor apartments equipped with climate control, floor to ceiling windows, and various other accoutrements of the modern era while Joe must make do with his 25-year-old cargo van, where he has a mattress in the back to sleep.

Furthermore, when the banks fail, the government helps them recover. Billions of Joe's tax dollars go to prop up the bank, yet Joe gets almost nothing from the government because he doesn't have a permanent address anymore. It is easy to see how the financial world can be viewed so negatively by so many. This is compounded by the fact that often those people do not understand how finance works. In a nod to the positive, prestigious side of the business, it is all a bunch of numbers and dizzying equations that are evaluated and decided in milliseconds by computers that seem completely cryptic.

There is a reason the government bails out the banks, though. These institutions are extremely important for the economy. Vast swaths of wealth are traded every day through the financial exchanges, and all of this makes those gleaming new towns possible. It enables a greater standard of living for the populace. Indeed, there are some estimates, quoted by reputable sources like Investopedia, that put the global derivatives market (under which options fall, but it is not entirely options) at 1.2 QUADRILLION USD – that is $1,200,000,000,000,000. That unfathomable number of dollars is a representation of what is traded around the world. If the banks were to suddenly vanish, the way the world works, with its consumerism that fuels trade links between political adversaries and crisscrosses the planet, would grind to a halt and everything about our modern life would simply stop.

Now, more about that derivatives market. Derivatives are a set of financial tools that derive their value from another, real source. During the financial crisis, it was about Collateralized Debt Obligations and Credit Default Swaps (high finance also employs arcane names). Another type of derivatives, much more understandable to the layman, is the option. Everyone knows how stocks work. Options get their value from stocks, and the most basic versions are easy to understand. Anyone can use options to make money, or, as we'll see, protect their investments against loss. The next few chapters will help you develop an understanding of what options are, how they work, who uses them and why they use them, and how you too can use them to either make or protect your money.

CHAPTER ONE

WHAT ARE OPTIONS? WHO USES THEM?

BASIC BASICS

If we make the division of the financial markets to a pricing, we will notice that there are two forms. Direct formation of the current prices of financial instruments, or direct settlement operations by making the trade or business in the current (spot market) market, which does not allow the significant deviations in the price of real demand and the formation of a high volume of speculative profits. Another division provides financial market characteristics of the futures market (forward market) whose operations include delayed execution of obligations of sellers or buyers. In this case, participants in trade are committed to a specific treatment in the future, taking into account the presumed relationship between supply and demand. This method allows the trade participants in their investment decisions incorporate the expected difference between the price movements of financial instruments in the current market and its expectations of future price movements in the forward price, and using the difference between these two prices, protect revenues and a profit / loss.

Futures derivatives market is a segment of the financial market, which owns and futures contracts denominated in the delivery of goods in the future. On this market, the department and financial derivatives are operating through forward contracts. The price of futures contracts is conditioned by the price movements of goods and financial instruments which are located on the grounds. Price follows - derived from the price of goods and financial instruments. Therefore, forward instruments are called derivatives.

Derivatives are financial instruments whose price is caused by the movement of goods and the price of the underlying financial instrument. Derivative securities or financial derivatives are very important instruments of financial instruments that have been incurred as a result of financial innovation in the last 25 years. Their appearance gave a new dimension to the stock exchange operations, leading it to major changes in the financial markets of developed countries, but also in the international financial market. As already mentioned, derived securities are called by their name because their value is derived from the value of some other underlying assets, which is located behind them. But in contrast to the basic securities, financial derivatives do not mirror any of the two main relationships: the credit and equity. They actually represent a particular type of contingent rights to other forms of financial assets (stocks, such as or other underlying securities, interest rate, market index, the exchange rate).

The real reason of financial derivatives lies in the growing scope and significance of futures transactions on the financial markets. The last 25 years have seen great expansion but their history is much longer. The roots of their business can be found in the 17th century on the territory of the Netherlands and Japan. First operations with financial derivates took place on the London Metal Exchange. These contracts were between buyers and sellers for the delivery and payment in the future, and they provided that the price and terms of payment had been negotiated much earlier, ie. on the day of signing the contract. These agreements were based on complete autonomy will of the parties, and there was no institutional mechanism nor they were standardized.

Side by side to this tradition, Chicago was developing the same market principles between the dealers. They introduced the improvements in the financial forwards and announced the standard amount (eg. For 5000 wheat bushels, as it is today). Chicago introduced standardized delivery during certain months, and in 1874 first clearing house was established at the Chicago Stock Exchange trading as a guarantor of delivery and payment. Options are certainly one of the most successful financial innovation even they were occasionally forbidden by some of the most developed financial markets. Forbidding the options happened in England between 1931 and 1958, and in the United States, between 1930 and 1973. The arguments of these restrictions were based on the point that options raise speculative character, or that they do not have the rational economic function when it comes to the case of the commodity. Organized trade options starts in the US in 1973, when based option exchange (Chicago Board Options Exchange) was established at the Chicago Mercantile Exchange (Chicago Board of Trade. The formation and organization of special market options allowed the operation of a secondary market that had previously existed to stay only as a counter market. Today the volume of trading options on the stock options in Chicago has surpassed trading volume on the New York Stock Exchange.

Over the last fifty years, futures and options took very important place in the international market. Originally futures and options were used on the stock exchange goods, and in the early seventies, their implementation also began on financial instruments. Currency futures experienced the expansion by the drop of Bretton Woods system of fixed exchange rates. The fall of this system announced new financial instruments to be used as in sense to reduce risk in the increasingly unstable environment. Options are traded on futures markets. The futures market obligated participants to trade on a specific treatment in the future, which means that the exact time in the future, may be determined by the day and the period of time depending on the type of contract that one party to deliver the assets in the contract and the other party pays the agreed cash amount. The agreed amount of money for which is made delivery of contracted assets, represents the futures price, which corresponds to the relation of supply and demand in the futures market. The contract which is concluded on the futures market represents, in some way, a bet between the participants in the trade about the future movement of assets with traded. The trading that is typical for futures markets provides an opportunity for participants to, when it comes to their investments, protect against unwanted price movements on the current market and thus in their investment decisions incorporate the expected difference between the price movements in the current and futures market.

Options are, in a single world, derivatives. What are derivatives? They are financial instruments that derive their value from underlying assets. In some cases, derivatives get their value from other derivatives, which increases the complexity, but the majority of traded options for you and me would be regular options on real assets. The most common type of option, which every finance student would learn about in an undergraduate finance program, is one that uses a stock in a company as its underlying asset. As finance may have some arcane names, they are usually not very creative. Options are so-called because they give you an option to do something: you can exercise the option before its expiry or not, and the exercising of the option carries with it a set of rules that must be followed upon execution. Most often this is a required buying or selling by the writer of the option.

So how do these options work? As in any transaction, there must be at least two parties. In options, there is the writer (or seller) of the option and the buyer. The buyer purchases the option and pays a small fee to the seller; the buyer then has the right to exercise, or execute, the option and its attached conditions before or on the exercise date (depending on the type of option). This fee is called a premium, and in many ways can be construed as the price to pay for the future ability to do something. However, true to the name, the option can go past its expiry date (i.e., expire), and the buyer can choose to let its value go to zero. Allowing the option to expire without exercising it is one of the very attractive features of the financial instrument. No need to do something after purchase if it does not go in the buyer's favor. The only loss is the small fee.

It is best to see an example, so, first, let's look at the most basic option so we can see how one works before we get into the more complicated or less intuitive types. Furthermore, let's only take the first example from a buyer's perspective, as one starting out should stick to buying until he/she has more experience. Selling options are a great tool to generate profit, but for some types the potential losses are, theoretically, unbounded and therefore are risky for those who don't know what they are doing.

As a buyer, we will buy a call options contract on stock MSFT (that's Microsoft). A contract is a pool of 100 options, so when you buy one contract, be aware you will be purchasing 100 instruments to use. The premium you pay, say 0.02/option or $2 for the contract, will go to the seller. This premium can be thought of as the price of the option. There will also be a category, expiry date, and a strike price. The category will be call or put, where call gives the ability to receive shares and put gives the ability to sell shares. The expiry date is, of course, the date by which you must exercise the option or let it die. For American-style options, you can exercise the option any time before this date. For the European-style options, you can exercise it only on this date. The strike price is the price at which you can buy the underlying asset, which, for us, is 100 shares of Microsoft.

So we bought our call option for $2, and we can exercise it before the exercise date. What does exercising entail? Say the strike price is set at $20 and Microsoft's stock price is at $19.50. If MSFT stock stays below $20 until the expiration date, then we will not exercise, and we will lose our two dollars. However, say MSFT's stock goes to $21.50 a few days before the expiry date. As stated, we have the option to buy, or call, 100 shares of MSFT at $20/share. We exercise the option and pay the seller $20/share. We can then either hold onto the shares, or, as many investors do, sell the shares immediately to the mark and lock in our $1.50/share, or $150 for the whole contract, profit. That is the most basic call option from the buy side. As with everything in an industry like finance, things can get extremely complex rather quickly, so in the next few chapters there will be the more common types, but I will throw in some complicated ones to marvel at – or to trade if you feel confident.

WHO USES OPTIONS and WHY

The possible money to be made, $150 on a $2 investment, is great. Usually the pricing and market don't work out that way, but sometimes it may. So who would use these things? The first obvious answer is speculators. People who are gambling on the direction of the market. It is easy to see how someone who wanted to gamble on the market could find appeal in a 7500% profit. And rest assured, there are plenty of speculators who trade options. Even if one does not have a lot of capital, a simple $2 gamble is cheaper than a lot of slot machines, and to many people it seems more legitimate to crunch some numbers and try predicting the future direction of the market.

There are others who use options in a more calculated and practical way, though. Options can be used by investors to hedge their investments. Hedging with options is like taking out an insurance policy on equity (stock) holdings. One simple way to see this is by looking at an investor who has 100 shares of Apple (AAPL). The put category of option (as opposed to call), allows one to sell shares at a specified price. The investor buys a put option contract and retains the right to sell the shares at the strike price, regardless of market price. This can be useful for long-term strategies. Let's give an example. An investor buys Apple stock (AAPL) at $30 and intends to hold it for the long term. However, due to some uncertainty with Apple's supply chain, the investor wants to make sure his entire portfolio does not drop below a certain price. The investor can buy a put option, which affords him the right to sell at a certain price, at $29. The option costs $2. Now, if the price falls below $29, the investor can sell. Why wouldn't he sell at $28.90? Well, first, he believes long-term the strategy is good. But if market conditions change, perhaps he will want to sell later, but by that time, the price has been hovering around $22 for three months. It isn't looking to come back up. He can still exercise his put option to sell at $29/share, locking his losses down to $1/share. The cost? $2. It brings him peace of mind to know he will only lose $1/share, and paid $2 for that protection, rather than to wait for the price to go back up, which it may never. On more less liquid stocks, prices may also jump from $30 to $25 (AAPL is nowhere near that low level of liquidity), but the put option holder still has the right to sell at $28/share.

One more example for hedging is during earnings releases. Earnings misses can often drop prices 10% afterhours and may even start a downtrend on the price of it. If an investor holds shares and expects good earnings, she may not want to sell. However, to protect her investment against a major downturn overnight from surprisingly poor earnings, she may buy put options contracts at 5% below the current market price. Even if earnings are poor and the price drops 10% and starts trending down, she only lost out on 5%. Hopefully, earnings will be as expected and her stock itself will increase, but that small premium for insurance is helpful for calm demeanor (essential for investing/trading), and her portfolio has a guaranteed maximum risk for that stock.

Often aggressive or institutional traders will hedge with options. Institutions may do so because they are required by law or they promise customers a maximum risk level. They can still take slightly larger risks and have a small premium for insurance.

The set of aggressive traders (of which institutions may also be members) can take large risks and wait for large gains while simultaneously holding risk at an acceptable level. It won't be zero, and the insurance won't be free, but the risk is mitigated and the traders can carry on without worry about legal requirements (specifically for heavily leveraged accounts) or losing their entire capital pool.

Options become much more complicated than this, and because there are so many varieties and strategies, one can hedge against almost any market condition. If one prefers, one can use options to play the market. Speculation can yield huge profits without putting up huge capital reserves. Small time investors can speculate (though some brokers do not allow brand new customers to trade options until a minimum experience is met) because options have implicit value. This is a function of the current market price, the strike, and the expiry. If an option's strike is about the current, but they are trending together, the price of the option moves up (another strategy to discuss later), and once the option goes "in-the-money", the investor can borrow cash from the broker for the short timeframe it takes to buy the option, turn around, and sell it back. Often investors just sell the option contract itself, as the price appreciates due to implicit value.

It ought to be noted that these options give you the right to buy or sell, but they do not give you outright ownership in a stock. Hence dividends and voting rights are not an option holder's right until the time the option is exercised and the stock actually transacted. This means a trader hedging the earnings report and dividend announcement won't be able to take advantage of a positive dividend because the ex-date for the dividend is before the announcement date.

You should now have a basic understanding of at least the very plain options, the concepts behind them, and who uses them for what purposes. Whether you are a speculator or a hedger, you will still learn about different strategies and the more complex options in the coming pages. With experience, adding options to your trading strategy is certainly a good way to add some extra revenue to your portfolio's revenue stream. The first thing to do is to look at how these things technically work. It is worthwhile to understand who the system functions before investing.

CHAPTER TWO

A MORE TECHNICAL LOOK

Options are a group of conditional derivative contracts, which means that they are derivative financial instruments. The main role of derivatives in the financial market is the transfer of risk. Therefore, there is a commodity or a financial instrument, or any assets that have marketability, and from whose price depends on the price of derivatives that are traded on the derivatives market or futures market. Many derivatives are used to reduce risk. For example, a farmer who is not sure what will be the price of corn at harvest and sales. To remove this uncertainty, it is protected by derivatives of corn future prices fall, thus avoiding the high losses. The basic role of the derivatives is the transfer of risk to participants who are willing to accept that risk and achieve huge profits / losses, as their forecasts of future price movements opposing those who want to protect themselves from risk. Participants who want to protect themselves from the risk are called hedgers, and those who accept that risk, and by realized profits / losses, are called traders (traders) which are popularly called speculators . Exchange-traded options include the right to buy or sell an asset, and the ability to withdraw from this right are the basic elements that make difference between the options and futures.

The futures market or the market of derivatives would not be able to function, without a large number of speculators who are always willing to "gamble". Some financial institutions tend to use derivatives as a source of income. This is a general reason of famous incident involving the collapse of Barings Bank in February 1995. But not just Barrings Bank dealt with difficulties. Great financial difficulties also had Procter & Gamble, Orange Country, Hammersmith and Fulham Local Authority. In the case of Barings Bank, Nick Leeson was obviously trying to take advantage of small differences in the prices of financial instruments which he bought on the stock markets of the Far East and sell them in other markets, trying to use a process known as arbitrage. In January and February 1995, he bet on Japanese stocks by buying a significant amount of futures contracts on the Nikkei 225 index on the stock exchanges in Osaka and Tokyo. There was a difficult period on the Japanese stock market which resulted in the disaster of the Barings Bank.

Options are the right to buy or sell a particular subject, such as stocks or government bonds at a predetermined price within a specified time limit.

the right to buy or sell an asset, and the ability to withdraw from this right are the basic elements that make difference between the options and futures. Futures involve the need to sell an asset, on a certain day, at a specified price, if previously did not "come out" of the contract. An option is considered to be a contract between the seller and the buyer in which he holds the right to buy or sell a financial instrument at a certain period of time or on a specified date in the future at a price specified at the moment of conclusion of the contract. The subject of the contract contained an option is called the basic investment (underlying asset). The subject of the contract can be:

• goods (commodities) - agricultural products such as wheat, oil, wood, various metals ... • currency (currency)

• Action (stock, equities)

• futures contracts (futures contracts)

• stock indices (indexes) the price of the contract which is determined at the time of conclusion of the contract or the price at which the assets, which is the subject of an optional contract, may be bought or sold, is called the exercise price (strike price, exercise price). The strike price or exercise price of those options is usually very close to the current price of assets and it is subject to an optional contract, except in cases of exceptional growth or falling prices.

It is because the stock market is determinating the strike price based on various analyses of the current market. Options are available in several amounts above or below the current price (current price, spot price) of the underlying investments. For example, stock prices that are below $ 25 per share usually have strike prices in the range 2½. The strike price of shares above $ 50 is generally in the range of $ 5. As for the share option, they are not available in every action. There are about 2,200 shares on which options are traded. Options are traded on stock exchanges around the world: LIFFE (London International Financial Futures and Options Exchange) -London, CBOE-Chicago, EUA-European stock market option, MONEY-France, and Deutsche Boerse and Eurex (German-Swiss international derivatives market) have opened a segment dedicated to the American actions. The opening of new markets in the segment of the Deutsche Boerse is intended to the best American actions-Xetra US Stars. Here we can find all the US stocks from the Dow 3ones Industrial Average, the S & P 100, Dow and NasdaqlOO 3ones Global Titans 50. On the same day, Eurex introduced options trading on stocks on denominated in the euro at 10 US stocks. These US stocks on which options can be found are AOL Time Warner, Cisco Systems, Citigroup, EMC, General Electric,

IBM, Intel, Microsoft, Oracle and Sun Microsystems. The introduction of options on the most liquid US stocks, helped the Eurex to develop an even greater extent in its segment of options trading. Derivatives based on stocks are offering a significant increase in value and have great potential for growth. Investors are expecting from the leading stock markets to offer intelligent products for derivatives based on stocks, as well as for the American risk management instruments. London International Stock Exchange of futures and options-LIFFE announced that the total turnover of non-financial products traded in October 2001, was 16% higher than the same period last year. They traded with 395,103 contracts, compared to 341,249 in October 2000. The traffic increased in September when it was traded 369,464 contracts. The largest percentage of growth was recorded at the trade agreements with the ground in barley and coffee. Vendor of the options, or actually the side of the contract which must implement its obligation, in the case that the buyer (purchaser/ holder) of the option wishes that the contract to be implemented, is called the issuer. The date in the contract that represents a term in which the option matures and after which no longer applies is called the expiration date, and it is usually the third Friday of the month when the option expires. Expiration dates can vary from one month to three years in the case of LEAPS (Long-term Equity Anticipation Securities) options. If a customer wants to use the rights that the option provides, he has to pay an appropriate price, which is called the premium (premium). The premium is the price of an option and it is determined by many factors such as type of the basic investment, the current price, the rate of price volatility of the underlying investments in the previous year, current interest rate, the strike price of the option, and the time remaining until the expiration of the option. In a case of share options, the premium is calculated by the per share method. Each option correspondent with the number 100. So, in case the premium is $2, the total premium for an option would be $200 ($ 2 x 100= 200$).

For example-

Let`s say that you want to buy a house. After few weeks of search, you found the house that suits you best. Unfortunately, you will have money to buy this house only in six months. Therefore, you will negotiate with the owner of the house and agree to buy it within six months. In this case, the owner sells you an option for $2,000. For the next six months, we have two possible scenarios. The first scenario is the possibility that the value of the house remarkably increases because, for example, they found the oil below the estate. However, the owner of the house is obligated to sell you the house according to the option you have bought and you have a right to sell this house and make a big profit.

The second scenario might be if you, for example, discover some toxic waste at the property you want to buy. Now, the value of the property decreased to 0 and you have a right not to choose the option to buy this house. In this case, you will lose $2,000 you have already paid, but you are not obligated to buy the house.

Besides the possibility to take advantage of the option until its expiration date, or not to do so, the buyer has the right and option to cancel the option (offset) .Offsetting is the procedure reversed from the original transaction, with the aim of leaving the trade. In the case of buying the call option, you should sell a call option with the same strike price and expiration date. In the case of selling the call option, it should be sold at the same strike price and expiration date as well. The same goes for the put options. In the case of buying, put options should be sold the same way with a strike price and expiration date. Analogously, if you sell put option, you need to buy a put option with the same strike price and expiration date.

There is a difference between European, American and Asian options. Attributes of Asian, American and European (Asian, American and European style) should not be brought in connection with the geographic locality, although most of the features on U.S. stock exchanges are the American style options. A European option is specific because the right of the option can be used only at maturity day. If the right of an option can be implemented throughout the entire period until maturity, then we are talking about the American style option. The maturity day or the expiration date is the last day when the holder is allowed to exercise it according to its terms. In practice, the European option is rarely used. Asian options are also rarely encountered, on the horizon that they began to trade only from 1994 on the CBOE. Asian options include the right, but not the obligation, of the buyer to buy or sell contracted assets at market price, which is derived as the average of its spot price at the agreed intervals. Asian options are related mostly to oil, metals and a certain group of currencies. All options of the same type (put or call) which have the same basic investment are called class options . For example, all of the call options on IBM constitute a class option. All of the options that are in the same class and have the same strike price are the call option series. For example, all IBM call options with a strike price of 130 (and different maturities) constitute a series.

There are two types of options contracts. The contract which contains the right of the person that buys the options and the appropriate assets in the contract at the strike price until the expiration date is called a call option or a stake (call) option. Another type of options relating to the contract that gives the buyer the right options to sell basic investment contract after strike price until the expiration date. Such an option is called a put option. Rights which are provided by call and put options, imply the existence of the other contracting party which agrees to make payments under the contract, to be implemented by the law. The second page of the contract is called vendor options. If it is a seller of the call option or the seller rights to "some" buy, then we can talk about counterparty that sells the right to set price (premium) to buy from it the subject of optional contracts at a price of execution. Seller shall, at the request of the buyer of the right to it is realized, the subject of the contract to deliver the well-established schedule. In the case of a put option seller or the seller the right to sell "something", then we can talk about the contract page that sells the right to set out the premium that it sells an optional subject of the contract at a price of execution.

You have a basic understanding of how options work, but how does all that math come together to make up prices. It wouldn't make sense if the strike price, expiry, current price, and premium together gave you a profit immediately after buying. That is called arbitrage and is relatively rare in well-developed markets; following the advent of computerized trading and deep interconnectedness, it is even more rare to find an arbitrage opportunity as all the information is out there and available to computers that can close the tiniest arbitrage in fractions of a second. So how do option pricing and the actual transactions work?

BASIC ELEMENTS OF THE OPTIONS

The agreed price of the substrate (strike price) is the specified price at which the holder of the options, can exercise his right to buy or to sell at any purchase or any sales, the base material which is backing options and the transition to the forward contract (price of goods at where the transaction will be executed if it comes to that).

The actual value (intrinsic value) is the actual value of the options which is determined by the difference between the contracted price of the substrate options and the current market price of the material. This means that the purchase option has real value if there are a price lining options below current prices on the futures market for the material.

Optional right means that it is not worth od using it if you use the option has no real value. Option to gain money – in the money, at the market terminology means that option has real value and it makes sense to use the optional right. The option of loss (out of the money) at the market terminology means that the option has no real value and that it does not make sense to use the optional right. Option at the money in market terminology means that the agreed option price is equal to the price at the appropriate time and it does not make sense to use the optional right.

The time value is a term expressed in value or the price that someone is willing to pay for a given option over its real value This happens when it is expected that adequate futures price material will change in direction that increases the real value of the options during the period of validity of the options. Since market sellers and buyers are both present at the market, premium, which consists of the sum of the time and actual value, also determines the price at which sellers are willing to accept the sale of optional rights.

Optional premium (option price) is, in fact, the price of an option. The premium option price is formed freely in the options market, based on the supply and the demand. Achieved premium is when the buyer pays the seller of the option for the right of the option which he gets by purchasing the option.

Options are traded in the same way as futures. The main difference is in the necessary security.

The holder of the options pays immediately the full amount of the premium to the seller of the option. He does not claim any security nor he is subject to any call from clearing house to provide the security.

The seller of the option, on the contrary, must give a certain security and he is exposed to the constant require and obligation to harmonize the amount of security at the invitation of clearing houses, identical to the mechanism that operates with futures markets in line with movements in the prices of the base material. Once the seller sells the option, If the option is in profit, he is exposed to the possibility that the option right, which he sold, turns against him, so his margin account at the clearing house should cover the amount of the loss of the option. Reconciliation is done on a daily basis.

EXECUTION (LIQUIDATION) OF THE OPTIONSMost of the buyers or sellers choose to liquidate the option or its optional position by canceling the purchase of the option by buying another, opposite option either at maturity or before the period of maturity.

As the buyer of the option activates the optional right only if the option has real value, this means that vendor options at the appropriate time, after activation of the option, suffers loss. However, this loss does not automatically mean that the vendor option will have a real loss. From this loss, he is protected by the collected premium, which may be higher than the loss of the option activating.

OCC-The Options Clearing Corporation is an institution based in Chicago, which was established with a view to ensuring compliance with the conditions of the option contract and the execution. Before they formed stock options and the clearing corporation option, the option holder who wanted to make the option, dependent on the ethics and integrity of the financial option seller or his brokerage firm. In addition, there was an appropriate way to close positions prior to the expiry of the agreed period. Corporation for clearing option as a joint body performs clearing the basis of all transactions with the options that are governed by regulations issued by the Commission for Securities and Stock Exchange (SEC- Securities and Exchange Commission). If the holder of the option chooses to exercise the right of the option contracts and that: a) buy (in the case of a call option), or b) sell (in the case of a put option) the basic securities that are the subject of the option contract, he must give an order to his broker who will deliver this order to the Options Clearing Corporation. To ensure the exercise of the option on a certain day, the option holder has to submit an order to his broker before the deadline for receiving instructions to carry out the options for that day. Different companies may have different deadlines for receiving instructions from the client, depending on the class of options. Upon receipt of the order for execution options, The Options Clearing Corporation randomly assigns the order for the execution of one or more brokerage firms that are in a short position in the same series. The brokerage firm, in turn, determines one or more of its clients, a random, was based on "priority" (First In First Out), which take up short positions in these series. The seller of the option that has been awarded an assignment for execution is required to sell to(in the case of a call option) The Options Clearing Corporation or to buy from it (in the case of sales), basic option. through his brokerage firm, under the strike price.

OCC-The Options Clearing Corporation, as an intermediary, shall provide either the delivery of the options (in the case of a call option) or pay a stipulated amount (in the case

put options) to the brokerage firm which is representing the holder's option, who exercised his right from the option contract.

The option premium is the sum of the actual and the time value of the options.

Premium = actual value + time value

When an option is at the loss its premium reflects only the time values, and it varies from the validity period of the options and the length of time in which the optional right can be applied.

The actual value of the option changes during its lifetime, in accordance with a change in prices of material, but it is always the real time while the value of the options has a speculative character, and depends solely on the assessment of market developments. Of course, at maturity options, the premium is equal to its real value, since the time component is expired and there are no more possibilities for any changes.

PRICING

The price of an option is determined by several factors. The first is whether it is in-the-money, at-the-money, or out-of-the-money. The first one means the option already has the difference built in. Ex: a call option on MSFT for strike $15 when MSFT is currently at $20. If one were to buy this option, he/she could buy shares of MSFT at $15 and immediately resell them in the market for $20. $5 instant profit. Of course, this is taken into consideration, and the premium for the option is going to be over $5. At-the-money means the strike and current prices are same, so there is no immediate profit priced in, but it is close. Out-of-the-money means the strike price is below (above) the current for a call (put). Assuming a call option, if the strike is $10 and the current is $8, then the buyer can buy the shares at $10, but that is an immediate $2 loss! Out-of-the-money options have no strike/current price different built in. This difference is called the intrinsic value.

Another factor is volatility. This can most easily be illustrated with at-the-money options, but it applies to all three. The more volatile the underlying asset is, the more the option will cost. If the strike/current are the same, but the price moves a lot, then there is more risk and/or reward involved, so the value of this volatility is added. This is called the volatility value.

The last factor is about time. This goes hand-in-hand with volatility, as more volatility over longer periods of time implies less certainty on the current price on expiry day. This factor address the probability the option price will change as it approaches the expiry date. If it is one day until expiry, it is much more certain what the final strike/current difference will be and therefore much less time value. To see the other side, say a call option buyer wants a one week option and a six-month option. The seller of the option knows much better how the one week option will play out and can price it accordingly. The six-month option, on the other hand, is too far into the future to know the outcome with any sort of certainty, so the seller will charge a higher premium to satisfy this greater risk. The buyer is willing to pay said higher premium because she wants to have protection (think insurance) over a longer period.

A MORE MATHEMATICAL LOOK

Note: This section can be skipped without losing anything. It is for the more technically minded who want a little more of the math.

Possibly the most famous equation in finance is the Black-Scholes model. It is a mathematical model used to determine the price of an option and specifically a European style option (the one that can only be exercised on one date, not a time period). Certainly, all finance students know it, and it has been around for a while. It was published in 1973 and is still widely used, though most users will add some of their own tweaks to it. There are several assumptions that underpin the model and are required before it makes sense. The original assumptions included a riskless rate (in practice this can be something like a US government bond); the market follows a random walk but it has a drift and volatility included; there is no arbitrage (more accurate now than 1973 due to computerized trading networks); money can be borrowed or lent at any fraction at the risk-free rate mentioned above; one can sell fractions of stock and short selling is allowed; and there are no transaction fees such as broker fees or commissions. Of course, this isn't the real world, but it approximates it well enough. Well-known changes have been made to incorporate common and unavoidable real-world conditions, too, such as transaction costs and taxes.

The equation itself is a partial differential equation and describes the price as it moves through time. The formula, which is used to calculate the price at any given time point and with given inputs. It is reproduced below from the Wikipedia page on it:

$$C(S_t, t) = N(d_1)S_t + N(d_2)Ke^{-r(T-t)}$$

Where

$$d_1 = \frac{1}{\sigma\sqrt{T-t}}\left[ln(\frac{S_t}{K}) + (r + \frac{\sigma^2}{2})(T-t)\right]$$

And

$$d_2 = d_1 - \sigma\sqrt{T-t}$$

This is the price of the call option. A put option is based on the parity between put and call options. $N(d_1)$ is the cumulative distribution function of the normal distribution operating on the variable d_1, T-t is the time to the expiration and adds to the time value (and remember, this is for European options, so the expiration does not change), S_t is the spot price (current price) of the underlying asset, K is the option's strike price, r is the risk-free annual rate under continuous compounding conditions, and σ is the volatility (this is the volatility factor).

Once these are put together, the current price of an option, based off the probability associated with the spot/strike (intrinsic value), time, the risk-free rate, and volatility, is output. The main reasons this formula is so famous is that it is widely used, it works, and to the people who don't know about finance, it is daunting. However, it shouldn't be daunting to you, since you know the underlying assumptions and the basic concepts of how it works. If you don't care how the inner workings function, then you don't have to worry because all brokers will list the prices and, unless you're writing options, you won't have to know how to determine the price. It is determined for you.

For American-style options, one can use a binomial tree equipped with probabilities at each node that can determine the price. The nodes are the prices, and they are connected along the time axis. Each connection is a probability and based off these two pieces, the tree is created backwards (from multiple possible ending prices) to the first node, which will give the current price. This is done in a discrete manner, not continuously like Black-Scholes, but with computers, it is easy to compute a large number of ending prices and a large number of steps to get the current price.

THE PARTIES TO TRANSACTION: BUYERS AND SELLERS

It is easiest to see how buyers can use options. It is also advisable for those starting out to only be buyers, as for certain types of options sales can be extremely risky. Not all, and selling options is a way to make money on stock you already hold, but for beginners, only buying is recommended.

In the most basic sense, buyers receive the option to exercise, and sellers receive a premium for their offer. The buyer takes on insurance or a speculative position and can make a large amount of money from a good movement or lose just a little bit. The sellers are taking a little amount of money for their service. If done correctly, sellers can lock in guaranteed profits on stocks they already have – this is practical in a sideways market. A little revenue can be taken from assets held, and if the seller intends to keep the assets for a while, this is not a bad strategy. If the option expires unexercised, the seller keeps not only the underlying but also the premium the buyer paid.

Sometimes the sellers are called writers, as they write the contract which goes to market. The buyers are holders of the option. Sellers are more often big institutions that need to be more calculated in their risks. Often large companies with huge resources will park their money in interest bearing accounts overnight. This interest tends to be very low, but on a $300,000,000 account, they still may bring in $200. They make the $200 simply by moving the money to a bank willing to pay the interest overnight. It isn't much, but it is just one more way finance has become incredibly efficient. Holding assets long-term may not generate profit if there are no dividends, so selling options, in the expectation they will expire without exercise, can lead to a similar small revenue stream for the company or individual.

Factors that have influence on formation of the time value of options

Time-term of validity of options (Maturity)

In principle, higher premium means that the validity of the option is longer is a period because it is more likely that there will be a change in the price of goods on the futures market. When the option is near the time of its maturity, its time value is dropping, and at the deadline, it has no time value at all. Options are sometimes colloquially called misspent assets.

MARKET OPPORTUNITIES

Market opportunities is an advantage of price movements Optional premium is certainly higher in periods of price volatility because then the movement of prices on the futures market becomes arbitrary and difficult to predict. The premium that the seller options serve as hedging will certainly be higher in such case since it is the risk that the option won` be in loss is higher as well. In such cases, the buyers of options are willing to pay a higher premium than in circumstances where the market is stable, and the price movement small and predictable because they expect significant price changes. In periods of market instability, options and shorter periods of validity can have a higher premium than the option with longer periods of validity in stable market conditions.

THE RATIO BETWEEN CONTRACTED PRICES OF THE OPTIONS AND THE MARKET PRICE

This relationship also has a direct impact on the premium level. Given the highly speculative nature of trading options in practice, it happens that the options that are on their own, or have a longer validity period, due to its time value, tend to be more attractive than the required options that are much in profit or have short maturities. This is also because the first have lower premiums and a higher probability of price changes than the others, in which the premium is high (can not be less than the actual value) and the probability of price changes is less possible.

THE INTEREST RATE ON THE MARKET OF SHORT TERM INVESTMENTSInterest rates also have an impact on the pricing of options, although not in the scope of what previously given factors have. Since the purchase of an option is a kind of short-term investment, the premium must be harmonized so that options are an attractive market for investment and competitive. Elevation in market interest rates of short-term investments in safe options certainly results in a fall of premium rates on options due to making these speculative options more attractive and prevent capital flight to other markets such as government bonds and etc. This means that the same amount money can cover a greater number of options contracts. Conversely, with the fall in interest rates, the premium rate can and will grow.

Optional premium is based, in fact, on the relative value by which it is traded on the futures market. Drop or growth of the premium depends on and moves in parallel with the movement of prices on the futures market. The right to buy something at a price that is lower is certainly worth more and should be paid more than the right to buy the same at a higher price. Also, the right to sell something at a higher price is certainly worth more and should be more paid than paying for the rights to sell the same at a lower price. This is why the call option with a lower agreed price have a higher premium, or put option with a higher agreed price are worth of paying more.

The right to buy or sell options lies in the prepaid price orPremium. It is determined by the process of competition on the market and it depends on the rating of the issuer actions, height price action at the heart of options, volatility and prices, the maturity of options and the general state of supply and demand of option contracts.

It is difficult to calculate the value of options that will stand on the grounds of its market value. Because of the fact that the option is the right and not the future yield, as it is the case with stocks, but the right to buy a financial instrument that gives you the right to a future yield has seemed that is is impossible to calculate the value of the options. In other words, the value of the options is doubly mediated. With any variation in the price action, the risk of the option is changing.

Financial markets theoretics agreed that the value of the options must be seen in close correlation with the price action, the price of the option and the premium. Forms of mentioned correlation (eg. Call

options):

• share price is higher than the price of the option,

• share price is equal to the price of the option,

• share price is lower than the exercise price of the option.

The option which is "in the price" has a value equal to the difference between the share price and the price of execution of the option.

This difference is called the internal value of the options. The premium is always higher than the intrinsic value of the option because otherwise the arbitrage investors would buy options and perform the same. The difference between the premium and the intrinsic value is the time value of options and expresses the growth potential of the option price, which monitors the share price in the period to maturity of the option contract. Price option has an upper and lower limit. The lower limit of the value of shares is the value in which it is transformed, if not executed. The lower limit of the call option's is the value at maturity. They use two basic analysis model to calculate the theoretical value of the options: binomial model, and model-Black Sholes formula. Both models have the same methodology, based on the fact that the risk of the option changes whenever the price changes - and that the pattern of price action is, as shown by analysis of the stock market, an accidental movement which means that it is impossible to determine the expected cash flow that option can be achieved and calculate the theoretical value of an option.

Therefore, we must find a roundabout method of values fortifications of options. Constituting an analog financial instrument or portfolio that can bring the same equivalent options shall correspond to the difference between the market share price at the time the option is exercised and the present value of the exercise price of the option. Financial theory finds this equivalent in combination of investments in the portfolio and the use of the credit markets, or debt investors, because of the purchase of options, in fact, means to raise a loan for the purchase of actions that will be implemented at the time the options executing. In such circumstances, buying call option is equivalent to the purchase of the action, but that is partly financed on credit. The value of call option has therefore become equal share price minus the option price. What makes these models differ, is a static or dynamic approach to calculating stock price volatility on the basis of option and decisive influence on their value.

READING AN OPTIONS TABLE

The trading volume in options escalated over the years significantly. The main reason might be in the fact that more and more traders have learned of the assembly of possible benefits which are available in case of the use of options. The advent of electronic trading and data dissemination were also the very helpful factor when it comes to options trading. No matter if it is used for hedging, speculating on price direction, crafting unique positions that offer benefits or simply underlying stocks, indices or futures, the ideal key to success is to choose the right option or synthesis of options which are necessary if we want to create a position with aimed risk-to-reward tradeoffs. While in the old day's newspapers had a significant role with their financial sections and rows of illegible options, nowadays we can use a more sophisticated set of information and statistics. In case someone wants to trade with options, he should have knowledge of the most looked variables which are listed in option data:

OpSym: This range labels the underlying stock, the contract month and a year. It also designates if it is put or call option.

Bid (pts): This field shows us the latest price which if offered by a market maker for the purpose of buying a particular option.

Ask (pts) : This column is the latest price which is offered by the market creator in addition to buying a precise option. It is very important to understand the difference between Bid price and Ask price.

Extrinsic Volatility (IV) Bid / Ask (%) : This field will inform us about the value which is calculated by an option pricing model. It represents the level of expected forthcoming volatility based on the present price of the option and other option variables. These variables include the amount of the time before the maturity of the option, the contrast between the strike price and the actual stock price, as well as the risk- free interest rate. More premium will be built into the price in case the (IV) Bid / Ask (%) is higher. In case the (IV) Bid / Ask (%) is low, less premium will be built into the price.

Delta Bid / Ask (%) :This column represents a value which is calculated by an option pricing model. It represents the stock equivalent position for an option.

Gamma Bid/ Ask (%) : Gama Bid / Ask (%) is a value that shows the amount by which the price of the option is expected to rise or fall. This value is based only on a point of increase in implied volatility.

Theta Bid / Ask (pts / day) : Theta Bid/ Ask is a value that informs us about how much of the value will the option lose within one day.

Volume: This is a very simple field which gives us the information on how many contracts of a precise option were traded in the latest session.

Open Interest: This column shows us the value which indicates the overall number of contracts of an option which was opened but not offset yet.

Strike: This field indicates the price at which buyer of the option can bargain the underlying security, in case he chooses to exercise the option he bought.

CHAPTER THREE

THE TYPES OF OPTIONS

There is a wide variety of option types. You already know the two categories of call and put. Call options provide the right to buy the underlying at the strike price and put options afford the right to sell the underlying at a certain price. You also know that one of the underlying assets is stocks. However, that is not the only kind of option.

There are also binary options, index options, futures options, barrier options, and even options options (that's not a typo, they're called compound options and are those complex derivatives I mentioned earlier). There are more types of options, and if you can trade it as an asset, it is likely someone somewhere has written an option for it.

A major trend in the world, in the last fifty years, is globalization, which is the process of integration of national economies through mutual trade and financial flows. One of the sub-processes of globalization that is very noticeable is the integration of the financial markets around the world into a global financial market where businessmen from different countries can operate with minimal or no restrictions.

Overwhelming integration of financial markets in the world occurred in the 1990s. This was preceded by a process of development of financial markets during the '80s. This process is reflected in the deregulation and computerization, as well as financial innovation and engineering. During this period, there was a system development of financial markets, institutions, instruments, and services. Financial markets are continually taking place in the process of financial engineering.

This includes a process of constant innovation of financial instruments. In the last three decades, there has been the creation and rapid growth of a new generation of trading options that are referred to as exotic options. Exotic options have become popular in the early 90s on the financial market in the United States. They are the most traded on the OTC (Over The Counter) market, although some of them are recently listed on VANCINI stock exchanges. For example, quanto options are traded on the AMEX (American Stock Exchange) and NYMEX (New York Mercantile Exchange) traded with spread options.

Trading with the options on the stock markets represents only a fraction of the total volume of trading exotic options. Due to the lack of transparency in the OTC (Over the Counter) market of exotic options remains exotic for many investors, as well as for those who know the standard forms option. Most common users of exotic options are big corporations, financial institutions, investment funds and private bankers.

Exotic options for their present name in the works of Mark Rubinstein who, during the 90s, described many types of exotic options. He published a series of short articles that dealt with evaluation of exotic options based on the Black- Sholes-Merton model.

The term exotic options are used for all optional contracts which are not standard stock exchange contracts, those are options with non-standard assets, determining the exercise price, the mechanism of payment or the terms of execution. They are called non-standard or special options also. Besides being exotic options have great flexibility and a large number of less expensive options, compared to a combination of common options that would provide the same payment. The reasons for the evolution of vanilla options and the use of exotic options are:

1.Exotic options are flexible instruments, that are better adapted to the needs of investors. Depending on the need, new types of the exotic options can be created.

2. Establishing the new and improved mathematical models of investment banks have been able to construct instruments with value-complicated structures.

3. It is significantly cheaper to buy the exotic option with respect to a combination of common options wich have same characteristics.

4. All greater understanding of techniques and ways of use of options by certain investors such as corporations or managers of funds has led to an increasing use of exotic options.

5. Increasing competition between the issuer in the market in recent years has led to an increase in the number of exotic options.

6. Also, speculation is one of the important factors for the development of exotic options. The possibility to realize attractive profits by taking risks on the basis of forecasts of market developments is the motive of many investors to buy exotic options.

Exotic options are almost exclusively traded on the Over the Counter market, although there are some examples where exotic options appear at the organized exchanges. The reason for the lack of representation in organized markets is that there are only small quantities and non-standard instruments, ie, there are differences from contract to contract. Also, exotic options are complicated for evaluation. The world's major banks are a major factor in the development and organization of trade exotic options. The world's largest financial institutions are nowadays giving the great attention to the development of new financial products. Users of the exotic options are mainly investors who are well introduced to the market and financial instruments, and those who have extremely high credit rating:

1. Portfolio managers

2. Small investors

3. derivatives dealers

4. financial institutions

5. insurance companies

6. corporations and other non-financial institutions

Corporations use exotic options to generate cheaper sources of funding and to create a hedging structure so they could reduce the risk in the business. Many multinational companies are operating in the various markets where they meet up with different types of risks such as currency risk, interest rates, political and other risks. Exotic options are instruments that can accurately eliminate these risks, such as, Asian and basket options. Exotic options came to the fore because of the great interest of the corporations which are, particularly, interested in cheap hedging strategy.

Although there are a number of exotic options, and therefore their properties that distinguish them from ordinary options, the most common characteristics of these instruments are flexibility and adaptability. Also, each od the exotic options, adds a new feature that makes it different from the others, with the purpose of meeting the needs of the market, and market participants. The most important features that characterize specific kinds of instruments in this group are:

The dependence on the path of the price of basic assets;

The structure of payments;

The dependence on the duration of the optional contract;

The dependence on the variability of prices of basic assets;

The dependence on the correlation between the underlying asset;

Non-standard fixed assets.

A large group of the exotic options has the function of payment that depends on the price movement of underlying assets. Will the option be paid or not, depends on the certain periods of time. The basic price of assets moved to the conditions is provided by the optional contract.

An extreme example of options depending on the price movement of underlying assets is an option with the American way of maturity which will, depending on the price movement of underlying assets, be carried out before maturity options if an investor deems it in an appropriate time for this. Highly dependent on the path of the price movement of primary assets are the options with restrictions that have features same as the ordinary options with one exception, the activating price. While the price of the stocks is within the limits, this type of options behaves like normal options, but its qualities manifest when it reaches the border level, and activating prices.

Function payments with exotic options are often different from the one in ordinary options. For example, the digital option has a fixed payout, which operates on the principle of the switch. In the case of favorable events, option pays an agreed amount. In addition, exotic options may be discontinued payments during a period of time or payments that can accumulate over the life of the option. The function of the payment can be enhanced so that the payment which would have a standard option increases the application of certain coefficients.

In addition, hundreds of exotic options can have the European and American way of maturity, they also may have the irregular structure of the execution of which depends on the type of exotic options, or by agreement between the purchaser and seller of exotic options.

For example, options can be used on the designated date during the period of the options, the first of every month, or every quarter, as is the case with Bermuda options. Items that are dependent on the duration of optional contracts also have a strong correlation with the variability of price base assets. Thus, for example, with complex options variability cord twice on the value of the options. Indirectly affect the value of the option over the value of the options that represents an underlying asset directly on the value of the complex options. Exotic options may apply to more basic assets between which there is a correlation between price movements. It is this correlation that represents the basis on which option will set up their value.

Exotic options may have a non-standard underlying asset. There is also the possibility of taking the option for option. Also, as basic assets may be the weather. In this way, the option read on the air temperature and the number of sunny ie. snowy days.

Exotic options are divided into the following, groups:

- Exotic options dependent on the price movement of underlying assets,

- Exotic options with a modified payment,

- Exotic options dependent on the weather and the variability of prices of basic assets

- Multifactorial or correlation options

- Other types of exotic options

For options that depend on the price movement of underlying assets (Path- Dependent Options) payment at the end of the function is the continuous path by the heterojunction essential assets that are held during the period of the optional contract. The path cost of the base assets may determine not only payment but also its scope, as well as the structure of the options. The most important options in this group are options with imitations, look back options, scale options, cliquet options, shout options and Asian options.

Options with a modified payment (Payoff Modified Options) have the function of payment which has been modified with respect to the payment function in normal option. They have a discontinuity or sudden jumps in the function of payment. For example, digital options pay a certain amount or not. They are easy to evaluate, but it is difficult to execute hedging with them because of the change in the value of options which can be very sudden. The most important options in this group are digital options, contingent options, and stage options.

Time-dependent options (Time / Volatility Dependent Preferences or Options) represent a group of exotic options where the buyer has the right to define the specific characteristics eg, type of options- time or call as a function of time. The value of these options is particularly sensitive to the variability of the basic price of assets during the period and it does not begin immediately, but at some future time. This type of option is especially useful when it is expected that some events that are happening in the short term have an impact on outcomes in the future. This group consists of forward start options, the option of choice, complex options, and Bermuda options.

Multivariate options (Multifactor / Correlation Options) are options on more assets. They are known as correlation options. These options have the function of payment based on the price ratio of at least the two of the essential assets that are interrelated. This means that, when evaluating these options, one should take into account the mutual movement and the correlation of prices of basic assets. This type of exotic option has become very important with the globalization of financial markets. The integration of financial markets in the world has led to an increase in the volume of foreign investments where multifactor options have become an important instrument for hedging. The reference assets appear in stocks, bonds, currencies stock indexes, foreign exchange rates, interest stoma and various kinds of goods. Some of the most important options in this group are basket options, the Quanto options, spread options and exchange options.

In other types of exotic options, we can include second-generation exotic options. These options are generally a combination of characteristics of exotic options which have already been written off. These are new financial instruments that have been developed to meet the needs of investors, which occurred after the events in financial and other markets during the 90s. Here, we also include the options that have exotic assets such as weather options or pass option.

Exotic options are, as usual options, an instrument that primarily serves as a protection from risks, but today many of them are used for speculative purposes. These options give companies the opportunity to reduce their exposure to risk through dynamic hedging. The company would not be able to reduce the mentioned risk through the static hedging.

These options also allow companies to achieve risk management at a lower cost compared to the one when using ordinary options. This is achieved by eliminating the cost of protection against the risk that companies are not required, and which are provided by ordinary options. Exotic options combine different elements of protection from risk, thus achieving a specific instrument is an adaptation to the individual needs.

Today, the most traded are Asian options, options with limitation, basket options, digital options, etc. These options are applied to all markets, both in commodity, currency, stock market action, and with market interest level, energy, securities with fixed income and etc. On the stock exchanges of goods and energy Asian options are traded, as well as the options that have a restriction on raw materials, natural gas, precious and heavy metals. On the Stock Exchange of currencies Asian options, options with limitation and basket options and digital options are being used on daily basis. Spread options are very popular in the bond markets and interest rates. These are most often used for:

Purchasing the basic assets, where the investor wants to buy a specific amount at a predetermined price;

Protection from the risk where exotic options are hedging instrument;

Reducing the cost of hedging. In this case, exotic options are cheaper in comparison with a combination of common options that would give the same value at maturity.

Increasing return or as instruments of speculation.

Exotic options have the necessary flexibility that is needed in terms of the dynamic market where we are constantly faced with new situations which are seeking for modification of existing instruments. Through all of this we can easily see the need and advantages of exotic options.

BINARY OPTIONS

This type of option is very simple and, as finance does not have creative names, its name implies its nature. It is a simple option that gives a payoff based on a yes-no outcome. If the holder is correct, the holder gets (wins?) $100, and if the holder is wrong, the holder gets $0 (loses the price for the option paid). It is one of the most gambling like options, as one is saying the price will be a certain amount at a certain point in time, and if I am right, I get all the money, but if I am wrong, I lose all of it. The buy-sell dynamic is considered a zero-sum game because the money lost by one party is the money gained by the other.

We must emphasize that the binary options are instruments which allow trading on the basis of financial movements of the selected investment class. This term can be defined as a detailed financial price of the product that explicitly defines an accurate reimbursement to which person will be entitled, upon expiry of the trading process. Binary options are financial products that allow trade in a wide range of financial assets, including currencies, stocks, bit coin, and goods.

All that it needs to be done is to correctly predict the direction of prices of the underlying asset at a certain period of time, in order to achieve certain gain. Binary options are different from those at Forex because traders do not have ownership of investment classes in which they trade, they only try to predict the value of the selected class at a certain time interval. Binary options are the simplest way of trading with different investment classes. With these options only two directions of movements are possible- call and put.

When a trader chooses in which direction will the investment class move, he will immediately know the percentage of the potential benefits or loss. In the case that the trader assumes correctly the movement of the index and its change, the gain will be over 79% of the investment. In case that he did not assume well, the movement of the index gain will be $ 0. Binary options are nowadays highly developed, and they became the quickest and easiest form of trading, mostly because of the percentage of payments which can be particularly high in most of the binary options. Nowadays, binary functions made a great addition to the revolution of financials. Trading has never been faster, easier, more profitable and approachable to everyone, no matter on the canvas possibility.

Binary options, no matter if we define them as a basic financial instrument, or any other way, represent the most simple form of the participation in the modern market. Binary options are not attached to some particular geographic locality; they are rather global and know no boundaries. The only boundary we can meet, when it comes to binary options, is the time, because, in case someone decides to trade, for example, on Asian stock market, he has to follow its daily schedule.

Trading with the binary options is a new and contemporary way of online trading and it attracts more and more users every day. Binary options popularity is growing every day. The great advantage of the binary options is the possibility of calculating potential profit in advance, even before the investment. However, on the other side, binary options can also serve to reduce the potential risks thanks to its advanced tools which most of the brokers offer. This second thing might be even more important than the calculating the potential profit. Today, it is possible to entirely personalize trades in details, and separately determine its exact time of its maturity and type of the option which should be used in trading.

Most brokers offer an additional option which helps to follow successful and experienced traders. This is a great help to beginners because it offers them safer start in trading.

In the world of binary options possibilities for the realization of the incredible user experience are numerous. Binary options are a relatively new form of participation in the financial markets. Without much hassle, they provide access to the trade market to almost everyone. Although after the financial crisis, people have a negative opinion on the financial markets and there is an atmosphere of noticeable distrust toward investments, it is important to stress that without the participation one can not reach benefit either. Binary options are simple instruments through which traders use knowledge of technical and fundamental analysis of securities in order to assess whether the prices of some securities will rise or fall.

With the advancement of technology and the Internet tools for trading, binary options have also evolved. Among the global market participants are using the increasingly popular computer programs that use algorithms to achieve the benefit of the financial markets. Many of them use reports that are obtained through official channels, before the publication in the media.

Algorithms are using technical analysis or chart analysis, by established rules, to predict the point at which prices will go up. The algorithms follow the market for a long time and, based on previous trends, make calculations about potential movements in the future. Given the fact that many traders do not have the knowledge or the time to learn about options, the creation of software for automated trading is helping them to cover their needs by recognizing signals and offering positions to customers.

It is, however, highly recommended that the traders have at least a basic knowledge of prices, lumens, trends and securities which they trade, so they could examine the charts and focus the software into more profitable opportunities. However, it is also possible to trade exclusively using only algorithmic approach; this is a very popular between undecided traders and beginners. Binary options are limited in time, so traders can enable trading in various intervals, starting from just a few seconds (e.g. 15sec) until the end of the month. If the period of time is shorter, the risk is higher but, on the other hand, higher risk brings higher profit. Within options of a medium length, the most popular are those of 60 sec.

Besides the fact that user can choose a time interval, he can also choose the investment class too. Investment class can be in currency, goods, indexes or stocks. In addition to these two factors, a trader should choose the type of trading. The most popular are the high / low, also known as a call / put option. However, there are a number of other options that are ideal for the implementation of various types of strategies. Key stock exchanges with trading binary options are Nasdaq, NYSE, Cantor Exchange, Nadax and many other. All these stock exchanges are easy to use even for users who have not been using similar services before.

NASDAQ (National Association of Securities Dealers Automated Quotations) is one of the most famous American electronic stock exchanges with headquarters in New York. The initial owner and operator of the NASDAQ are The Nasdaq Stock Market, Inc. whose shares are also offered on their own Stock Exchange under the symbol NDAQ. Commencing in 2002, NASDAQ has nowadays become one of the largest online screen- based stock markets and it is used around the world. New York Stock Exchange / NYSE is the world's largest stock market for securities.

New York Stock Exchange dates back to 1972 and has passed through various stages of development until it became what it is today. NYSE is not a corporation and not even a partnership; it can be described as a voluntary association. The number of members of the New York Stock Exchange is limited to 1366. Members can perform a variety of functions that fall into two categories. One group of members is working on behalf of their clients, and the another group of members is doing business with other brokers and working for its own account.

These options have hourly, daily, and weekly expiry points, so if you don't want to wait a week for its expiry, you can buy one for the next hour. Remember, time value still plays a role here. Some are based on reports and press releases, so they will expire about the earnings report is released or some other similar event connected to the option.

The risk and reward are both capped. You will either make $100 or make nothing, but you can't lose more than you bought it for. With that in mind, if the stock price moves significantly in the next week, you may have been better off with a regular option. You cannot make more than $100, but if the stock moves up enough, a regular option may have netted you $150 or $1500. However, in sideways markets, it is easier to profit. If the most return on can get from the underlying is $50 overall on your capital and you go with a binary, you can double the payoff of the underlying market.

BARRIER OPTIONS

Another type of option that does not get a lot of attention but has interesting features is the barrier option. This exotic option carries two ways: knock-in or knock-out. As mentioned earlier (though yet to be demonstrated), one can lose much more money than put in if writing options in a risky way. Barrier options limit that risk. Of course, that also means the gains are limited. Knock-outs are the ones that protect the sellers. Here, an option becomes worthless if the underlying passes a certain point. Until that time it can be traded as a regular option, but once it passes the knock-out point, the loss is limited to the seller as the option "ceases to exist" and becomes worthless.

On the other hand, a knock-in option will "come into existence" once the price point is reached. As with all things financial, the direction can go both ways. On a down-and-in option (like a put), if the spot is $30, the strike is $27, and the barrier is $25, there will be no right for the holder to sell the stock at $27 until the price of it went below $25. If you have been following along and understanding, you can probably think of some investors who would be interested in such a strategy.

INDEX OPTIONS

Index options are based on an index (Dow Jones, S&P 500, etc). Indices are groups of stock that, together, give a return. Most of the index options are European style. Index options grant a trader usage of call or put options so he could gamble on the movement of an entire stock market index. These options allow a trader to take the advantage of their prediction of the direction or volatility of the entire market, rather than having to trade options on each particular security. One thing that is common for almost all the traders, when it comes to index options, is the challenge of calculating the estimated dividend. Index options are more stable than other types of the options because the index is liable. These options have much smaller chance of becoming a subject of volatility than the individual stocks and they are widely traded by hedge funds and investment companies, as well as the individual traders. The idea behind indices is to diversify the portfolio easily, so one does not need to research all the different companies for a good risk diversification strategy. They are also often used to gauge the health of the economy since some can represent the largest companies or a good breadth of various companies.

Like equity options, index options have multipliers. The buyer is not getting ownership in the index (or, indeed, the group of shares that make up that index) but instead is getting the representation of it. The underlying here is the cash level of the index. The multiplier is usually 100, so if the strike price is 600, that represents a $60,000 investment in the index. However, the price (premium) of the option surely will not be 600. It may be $15. In that case, the whole contract costs $1,500 and represents a holding of $60,000 of the index. The dynamic works the same as the other options: in-the-money, at-the-money, and out-of-the-money. If the spot price hits 610, then the profit is (610-600)*100 = $1000. Of course, this is actually a loss scenario, because the cost of the option was $1500, which implies the investor lost $500 on the trade.

MINI INDEX OPTIONS

Mini index options are very similar to the basic index options. However, mini index options have only 10% of the contract size, as well as only 10% od the cost. The fact that the cost is lower helps the traders with limited capital to gain a profit in trading on the global market. We can say that these options are acting like a replica of index options but with a difference that they offer a partial hedge against index options. These options have very often extrinsic value which can be very high because of their lower liquidity. However, mini index options are very often more expensive than the ETF options.

FUTURES OPTIONS

Futures themselves are interesting financial instruments. While options give the buyer the right to exercise but do not obligate them to do so, futures obligate both sides of the trade to transact at a specified price and date. Futures are commonly made on commodities so buyers and sellers can guarantee themselves acceptable prices and forget about the market risk. Think farmers who want to sell their crop in 6 months without having to worry about how the price will change and companies who want to purchase raw materials, see a good price now, and want to lock it in when they need to repurchase in a year. This type of instrument can have its own book written about it.

Similarly to the equity (stock/share) options mentioned before, futures options provide one the right to purchase an obligation. That may seem a little weird, but there are parties out there who would need such a setup. This is why finance can get so complicated: customized products built from other products, which in turn are built from further underlying products. Futures options are not focused on a lot, so we will leave it at that for now.

OPTIONS OPTIONS

Of course, why stop with indices or futures? They are both derivative in some way because neither is a real, tangible thing, but they both have options built off them. So, sure enough, Wall Street created options for options. This sort of compounding of financial instruments can be a risky business, especially because compounding tends to highly leverage positions. Nonetheless, there is a market for options on options, because there are some investors who believe that can handle the intricacies. Of course, as another layer of the chain needs to be calculated, it becomes a more laborious task that requires more sophisticated knowledge.

EMPLOYEE STOCK OPTIONS

One type of option that is not publicly traded is the employee stock option. They usually have a vested period, which means the option cannot be exercised before a certain date (to keep employees from getting their bonus stock options and disappearing). Just like regular options, these allow employees of a company to buy its stock at a certain price by a certain date (and after the vested period). They are used to motivate employees to work hard, which in theory will push up the stock price. With a low strike price and a high spot price, the employee can buy shares and then turn around and sell them for a profit on the open market. Of course, this is an option, so if the price falls, there is no reason to exercise the option.

An employee stock options can be a very profitable instrument of the investment if it is properly used. These strategies have a long tradition of the successful tool which attracts as the top executives as well as Non- executive employees. However, because of the incapability of taking the full advantage of these strategies, some people still fail in gaining the profit which is generated by their employee stock. The key to maximizing potential profit is to understand the nature of the stock options, taxation and the impact on the personal income. Employee stock option is presented as a contract which is issued by an employer to an employee with a goal of purchasing an amount of shares at a fixed price for a limited time. These shares are purchased at company stock. There are two main classifications of the employee stock options:

non-qualified stock options (NSO) are mostly offered to non-executive employees, consultants, and outside directors. These options do not experience special federal tax treatment so the grant is not a taxable event. The most important characteristic of the non-qualified stock options is that transactions within them must go through specific terms which are set by the employer agreement and the Internal Revenue Code.

Incentive stock options are reserved only for executives of the company. Incentive stock options receive favorable tax treatment since they meet very special statutory rules which are described by the Internal Revenue Code. In both of these options, employee stock option is admitted at the exercise price. Exercise price, in this case, is the price per share which employee has to pay to exercise his options. This price is very important because it helps to determine the gain and the tax which is payable on the contract. This element is called bargain element and it can be calculated by subtracting exercise price from the market price of the company stock.

ETF Options

These options are based on the exchange- traded fund (ETF). Exchange- traded fund options are an investment pool which is traded on the many stock exchanges. These options are available on almost all of the stock indexes and traded in the same way as shares of stock in publicly listed companies. A trader can buy or sell shares or o options of an ETF by using a brokerage account. One more way what ETF options can be traded is by selecting an industry which helps the trader to pay attention to predicting price movements of only one industry, instead of focusing on combined selection of stocks.

ETF options can be very advantageous when we speak about day- trading strategies such as hedging. In this case, the trader should be well knowledgeable and informed about the practice of the underlying security. When trader becomes confident and well- informed, he can make a profit from the low costs and tax benefits while trading with ETF options.

IRA Options

IRA options are known as Individual Retirement Account Options which can not be used for day trading because of the U.

S. Securities and Exchange Commission`s day trading rules. Ira options are limited to cash category accounts so it is impossible to act as a margin account. However, there is one alternative which is offered to IRA traders which consist of options which can be traded against the value of future contracts. In this case, there are no restrictions when it comes to day trading or futures options through an IRA account.

There are yet more types of options and, really, if one had the desire, custom options could be written. These would not trade on an exchange as there is not enough liquidity, and for some types of deals, it is perhaps better that the public does not have access. Transactions off-exchange on custom instruments make up a large portion of the derivatives market. Convincing a farmer to buy an option on his wheat is unlikely to happen (he is much more interested in a futures contract), but options do exist outside the traditional marketplaces for finance.

CHAPTER FOUR

THE TYPES OF TRADES AND STRATEGIES

You know about the basic option strategy, but I will reiterate it here for referencing convenience and so you can see how it works from different angles. Then I will lay out some more complicated ways to trade and use options, both speculative/money-generating and insurance styles. If you look online, you can find a lot more information and helpful charts (which I will not reproduce here) that give you a visual on entry and exit price points and profits. Most of these have an opposing strategy that utilizes the sale of options. I lay them out, but remember, writing options is risky, and the upside is comparatively small.

There are many strategies which one can use while trading with options. Let's think about the four scenarios and basic options strategies. Knowing that possession of a put option on the property give you the right to forward the sale of a commodity at a predetermined price, we can assume that the manufacturer of a commodity, such as, for example,a corn, wants to buy a put option at the time of sowing or during the development of corn with the intention to fix the selling price of the product at the time of the harvest.

Except for the amount of premium that is already paid, the purchase of such options will not prevent you from profiting in the case of price growth above the agreed level, which would be the case with a regular forward contract, or any form of forward protection in the futures market - hedge. Let us assume that the manufacturer of corn bought put option in May with the expiration in October and paid a premium of 0,010 $ / kg for the option with the agreed price of 0,270 $ / kg (option at that time was on its forward price for October 0,270 $ / kg).

The option gives him the right but does not impose an obligation to sell a corn at a price that is fixed in the option. This law applies to him until he decides to execute the option, resold or leave to expire unused (deadline for a decision is September). If in the meantime happens the fall of the October term from 0,270 to 0,250 his put option will have a real value of 0,020 $ / kg and this gain will cover the difference in price that occurred on the futures market. The result of this transaction would be:

• the purchase of put options for October contract price 0,270$, the premium paid - 0,010$;

• sale of the put option in October, the agreed price 0,270$, payment of the premium + 0.020$; • selling corn at the current price of + 0.250; -- -- --------------- total realized 0.260$ +

If it happens that demand for corn, at the time of harvest, pass the expectations, and significantly higher price for the October term increase to 0,290 $ / kg, the manufacturer will leave that option to expire without using it, and also offer premium paid, but will be free to sell the corn at the market for a higher price, or 0,290 $ / kg. The result then looks like this:

• the purchase of put options for October contract price premium paid 0,270$ - 0,010$;

• no use put options 0,000$;

• selling corn at the current price of + 0.290$

; -- --------------

total realized 0.280$

If manufacturer entered the forward transaction protection- hedging, or in case he entered just an ordinary forward contract, he would not have a chance to make a profit emerged as the result of growth in prices, which with the option remains a possibility.

Also, if it happened for any reason of force majeure (drought, city, fire, etc.) that the manufacturer lost his crops, an ordinary term contract - forwards - would remain him under an obligation to deliver the goods, while futures enable him to close the purchase of counter positions, which could be costly. The option helps to protect from such cases.

Let's look at this scenario from the position of the corn manufacturer at the beginning of the harvest. He does not want to sell an entire annual harvest of corn at the time when the offer is the largest and, consequently, the lowest price. He wants to leave some of the corn for the rest of the year when it is expected that the price will be higher and higher profits will be achievable. On the other hand, the manufacturer needs the money immediately, either to pay off some credit commitments, either to avoid interest on new borrowings that followed the start of a new cycle of production. In addition, there are also storage costs, while at the same time remains a risk that the price, for whatever reasons there might be, instead of the expected increase, starts to fall.

Probably the best solution in such case lies in the decision to sell the whole sowing immediately and, at the same time, to buy some options for one or more specific search terms. In this way, he immediately comes to the necessary resources, avoiding the expense of new debt, the cost of storage and the risk of a possible drop in the price, but at the same time, it gives him the opportunity to achieve profits from the growth of prices - which must be greater than the premium paid for the call option. Of course, the maximum loss that may follow such a transaction is the level of already paid premium, which is certainly much smaller loss, or at least limited in relation to a possible drop in prices and a theoretically unlimited loss, which may occur if he had the goods stored and wait for an appointment for sale. This example would look like this:

The manufacturer sells his fruit immediately after harvest, in October, at the current price of 0,250 $ / kg, without waiting for a possible later sale achieved at a higher price, but, at the same time, he comes to so the necessary funds.

At that moment, the forward price for May is 0,270$ and he decides to buy the May call option with an agreed price of 0.270$with a premium payment of 0,010 $ / kg. If in April, when May options reach, the price of corn as expected rises to, for example, 0,290 $/ kg, the options that he has will be the actual value of 0,020 $ / kg. By realization of the optional rights and reselling it he will achieve the profit of 0.010 $ / kg .

The sense of the selling options is prompt payment of the premium. This applies equally on the selling, as well as the buying and selling of options. Will there be a decision to sell or purchase put options, or even both at the same time, depends mainly on the financial potential and forecasts of price movements on the market. A call option is sold mostly by those who do not expect a significant increase in the prices of basic materials or those who think that the market trends when it comes to the growth of prices will not be so high to exceed the number of collected premiums.

If sold options expire without use, the seller will have a premium as pure profit. Suppose that in the time of harvest (October) manufacturer of corn estimates that the price of corn will be stable in the future and decides to sell the December call options. The price of corn futures market for the December delivery is 0,270 $ / kg, and in the options market in December call option with an agreed price of 0,270 sold per 0,010 $ / kg. If in November, when the option price, due to the prediction of manufacturers, remain at the level of 0,270 $ / kg, the option holder shall not use the optional right and manufacturer will benefit from the full amount of collected premiums.

The strategy of selling the call options on the basis of the owned goods (either on the field or in storage) is called covered strategy. This is because any kind of loss of the option due to rising prices is covered with about the same, but the positive, realization of the goods sold in the daily market. However, if there is a significant fall in prices, a commodity that is in the possession is protected only up to a number of collected premiums. It is also possible to sell the call options without coverage, or naked options, which means that there is no substrate in commodity assets. This sale is completely speculative and risk is potentially unlimited. If such an option is implemented, the seller is exposed to a loss for the full amount of the increase in commodity prices above the agreed price of the option minus a number of premiums collected. In these transactions, with uncovered options, can indulge just extraordinary market experts who are capable of taking the financial risk.

As stated above, profit from the collection of premiums is the main motive for the sale of options. Put options are sold by those who do not expect a significant drop in prices of primary materials - lining options.

For example, a cattleman who predicts that the price of corn will not change during rounds, can go to the market options to get out with his sales options. His main motive is that the cost of corn, which he will anyway buy in the future, reduce at least for the amount of option premium.

THE BASIC CALL/PUT STRATEGY

The first and most basic is to buy options to make money on the positive difference between the spot and strike prices at some point during the option contract's life. This is the strategy we have been discussing: you buy an option with a strike of $30 on GOOG with a current spot of $28, and if the price of Google's stock goes above $30 at some point during the contract, you can exercise. This ignores the cost of the option, so your profit on a call is really spot – strike - premium paid. Remember that there is also time and variation premiums that need to be accounted for, but you will be able to see the price of contracts on your trading platform. This trade has unlimited upside, as the stock price can theoretically rise without end, but you always have the option to purchase at a set price. The downside is limited to your premium paid.

On the other side, you can try a put option. This is similar to short selling: you want the price to fall. The put gives you the right to sell the stock at a set price, so you buy a contract (remember it is for 100 units of the underlying) for strike $30 with a current spot of $32 and wait for the price to fall below $30. Say it falls to $25, then you can exercise the option and the writer of the option must purchase your shares at $30, even though you can buy them on the open market at $25. This has limited upside, as the farther a stock can fall is zero. Hence the maximum you can gain is the strike price times the number of contracts times the multiplier (usually 100, for those 100 shares). Your downside is limited to the premium.

Those are both out-of-the-money examples. You may want to go with in-the-money contracts, where your option already guarantees a profit if you ignore premium. However, the intrinsic value of the difference will cause the premium to be significantly higher, and hence you will still need to wait for a price difference.

WRITING SIMPLE CALL/PUT OPTIONS

If you are certain the price will go a certain way, it is best to buy options. However, if you are holding shares already and want to make a small premium, writing an option may be an option for you. This is a strategy for a sideways market. An example may help: you own 100 shares of MSFT, which you bought six months ago at $15. The current price is $15.50, and the stock has been moving between $14.95 and $15.70. This isn't much profit, and you expect it to stay in a very small range. However, you like the dividends, so you want to keep it. You can make a small premium on it by selling options.

If you write in-the-money-options, you will get a higher premium, but there is a higher chance of it being exercised. At first, the premium will cover any loss you would take, so if the price stays close, in-the-money option writing isn't necessarily a bad strategy. Say you write a call option for $16, since you haven't seen the price go to $16 in the last 6 months and don't expect it to happen anyway. You get the premium (based off time, volatility, and intrinsic (which is zero here)). If the price goes above $16, then whoever bought your call may exercise it, and you will be forced to give them your MSFT stock. If, however, the price tops out at $15.80 during the life of your option, the buyer won't exercise it, and you will get to keep the premium. After it expires, you can write another one or go with another strategy.

As you can see, the loss is not necessarily a real loss. It is an opportunity loss. If your buyer exercises, you will be required to give them the designated number of shares and lose out on any profit you may have reaped. If MSFT jumps to $30, then you will lose that $14/share profit, as you have to hand over your shares for $16 instead of selling to the market at $30. Of course, you don't expect the price to move that much otherwise you wouldn't write the option!

The dangerous situation occurs when you write so-called naked options. If you already hold the stock, you have opportunity lost. With naked call writing, you are writing options on stocks you DON'T own. If you write a naked call as above, but never owned the stock, if the price of MSFT does indeed rise to $30, and your buyer decides to exercise then, you will need to buy enough shares at $30 to satisfy the contract. However, when you sell them, you must sell them at $16. Therein lies the problem: you can get locked into huge losses. Naked call writing does not even give you assets at the end of the trade. At least with naked put writing you can hold your newly acquired, very expensive shares until the price rises again (if it does). Naked put writing can be used if you are interested in owning more of a stock, are willing to take it at a certain price, and think the price will eventually rise. Not a bad strategy for long-term investors, but it still carries significantly more risk. Both are definitely risky and not advisable for new traders. Personally, I find naked call writing riskier than naked put writing, since you can at least hold your new shares. Further, naked puts are naked only because you are not holding a short position already. If you are holding a short position and write a put option, it is a covered put, not a naked put. However, holding a short position has its own set of risks, including having to pay dividends back out and the unlimited loss (on the short position, not the put option) if the stock price rises.

WRITING A NAKED CALL

The most common goal of writing uncovered or naked call options is to create cash inflows in periods in which the market is stable, but even though it seems that it is not difficult to find period when the price is steady, in the life of any futures contract, writing strategies for uncovered option is very risky. Specifically, with the increase in futures prices of goods, the value of the option is also proportionally increasing.

Warranty to meet the rights under the option is the margin deposit that is taken (each time) when it sells a call option. Thus, in the case when the price goes on the contrary to expectation and when you need more money to meet these rights, it could result in margin calls. And if it comes to the margin calls, it is recommended to, either accept the loss or invest more money. Investor sentiment is neutral or moderately "bear" in such case.

Therefore, it is expected that the price of a particular futures contract remains unchanged or to slightly fall. The aim of the investor is to make a profit, despite he estimates that in the next period, the market will be stable. The risk is unlimited if the price of this appointment contract, for the duration of the option, rise sharply. The value of options and losses, in this case, will continue to grow. Profit is limited to a number of premiums collected. Investor sentiment is neutral or slightly "bullish" in this case.

Therefore, it is expected that the price of goods that are traded in the coming period will remain unchanged or will increase a little. He aims to make a profit in the conditions when the prices on the market become stable. The risk is unlimited as long as the price of a given futures contract falls. Profit is limited by the amount of the premium for that option which is sold. Explanation of the strategy: If the price of goods, as well as the value of a forward contract, remain unchanged or increase slightly in relation to the cost impact of put options, option seller will make a profit. In case the price falls, the option seller will suffer loss.

STRADDLES AND STRANGLES

Suppose you expect the stock price to move significantly, but you don't know which way it will go. A good example is during earnings announcements. If the earnings are great, the stock will rise, but if they are terrible, it will fall. Of course, that assumes the market is expecting something tame, and the report is anything but tame. Can you still make money from this event? Of course!

The straddle is comprised of two parts: one put and one call. You purchase one call and one put at the same strike price with the same underlying and expiration dates. This ensures the profits from the opposing options move in lockstep. How can that make you money? First, if the price doesn't move significantly, then you don't make money. Your downside is the price paid for the options (which is double just a single option, as you must buy both sides). However, this downside is limited to the premium for both contracts. If the price drops significantly, then the losses on the call bottom out at the strike price, but your gains on the put can continue to rise. On the other hand, if the price jumps, the losses on the put are limited to the premium, but the profits from the call can rise indefinitely. This is why the price must move significantly: the profits from the one side must offset the losses from the other, but the losses are always limited while profit is not – though keep in mind put option profits ARE limited to the price falling to zero, so this may not work on very cheap stocks. The profit/loss line on the chart "straddles" the strike price, hence the name.

Another strategy using this concept is called the strangle. While the straddle will have at least one side in-the-money (the dynamics of the trade require this), the two sides to the strangle will generally both be out-of-the-money. This is possible because the strikes between the put and call are different. As usual, the downside is limited to the premium paid on both contracts. This premium is also much cheaper than the above straddle premium since the options are out-of-the-money and the intrinsic value will be zero. The dynamics are the same as the straddle, but you will need more movement in the underlying. Since both contracts are out-of-the-money options, it will take more movement for them to become in-the-money or profitable. This higher risk is offset by the fact that the actual capital at risk is less, as you won't be spending as much on premiums.

Does this trade have a selling complement? Yes, and it uses the other area of the chart to make money (the price staying in a small area). The maximum profit is the premium gained, but here you get a range for the stock price around the strike(s). If the stock moves significantly outside, whoever is on the opposite side of the trade gets the money (that would be you if you followed the above strategies). However, if the price stays within your calculated range, you get to keep the premium or some portion thereof.

SPREADS

Positions that are composed of at least two of the same options that have limited risks, but also limited gains, are called Spread strategies. These strategies can be horizontal, vertical, diagonal and box range. Vertical ranges include purchase and sale of an equal number of the same options with the same maturity date.

Depending on whether you bind on expectations of price change of the underlying assets or the level of its volatility, the spreads can be bull, bear, and wingspreads, and each one of them can be achieved by the call and put options. Each this spread must be made "in a package"

Without the possibility of carrying out individual options. the investor takes the strategy of the vertical bull and bear spread when he expects some changes in the price of the property, but, at the same time, he wants to restrict from the excessive losses because of which he is ready to accept the lower profit. He enters the position by combining one long and one short position in identical options as opposed to the relative amount of the underlying assets in which received a premium of short position reduces the cost of buying the long position. On the other hand, buying a long position reduces

Exposure to short positions. The benefit of the strategy is double protection - from increasing and by reducing the price. Such ranges could take more cautious speculators.

The horizontal spread represents the investment strategy being carried out simultaneously by taking long and short positions in the same type of option on the same underlying assets with the same time of maturity, but with different exercise prices. Depending on which options are used in the preparation of the horizontal range, we can see the difference between:

- Bull Call Spread

- Bull Put Spread

- Bear Call Spread

- Bear put Spread

BULL CALL/BEAR PUT SPREAD

A spread is a difference between prices. Here, the spread will be on the strike prices of two sets of options. As with the straddles and strangles, this will require more than one piece. This involves buying and selling in the same trade, but we will limit the risk on the option writing with this strategy. I will give you an example here of a bull call spread, but the same applies (using the converse) for bear puts.

The idea is to buy a call option below the strike price of your put. This can be in-the-money or out-of-the-money. The price points at which you buy and sell will determine how much you will make and how far out from the spot price you will go. For a simple example, we don't even need the spot price, but keep in mind the spot will have a large impact on your strategy and how much you can expect to make. The first step is to buy a call option, say at $50. Now you can sell a call for a higher strike, say $55. You can even do this naked without much risk. Your $50 call option can be exercised to get the shares and then sell them at $55 to your call option holder. This implies your maximum profit is the difference between the strikes plus the premium you got from writing the higher call. The premium from the writing is generally used to offset the costs of the lower call. Of course, if the price of the underlying remains below your lower call, that call expires worthless, and since your purchased call is closer to the underlying, the premium will cost you more than you will recoup from the call you sell. This type of trade is considered a debit trade, as you will always need to put up more money to buy the lower call than you will make from the higher call.

Winning outcome of bull spread is related to the increase in the price of the underlying assets, while the success of the bear spread is the expected substantial decrease in prices.

Bulls call spread is assembled in a way to buy a call option of underlying assets with a series of excellent prices and to sell the call options on the same property but with a higher strike price. The success of this type of spreads depends on the increase in asset prices and the fall in prices, which will cause a loss. In this way, possible gains and losses are limited.

The preparation of the strategy of a bull put spread starts from the same position as for the various strike prices, so the bulls call spread consists of purchasing put options with a lower price and a put option with a higher cost. In the case that the price increases one will achieve limited gains, while the price drop will cause limited losses. A great price depends on a price of the put option. An investor who has a strategy bull put spread has a range of credit because he earned money on the difference in price. The investor buys an option at a lower price but sells another option at a high price. That's why we talk about credit range. If prices rose above most strike prices, investors with bulls put spreads strategies will achieve the greatest profits. But in a case of price drops below the lowest strike prices, this spreads strategies will achieve a limited loss of premiums.

Bear Put Spread is a combination of purchasing put options on certain underlying assets with the higher strike price, as well as drawing up a put option on the same property with a number of strike prices. This strategy gain is realized in the event of falling prices since the investor has the bear's expectations. Maximum height loss and gain are limited. As in the above ranges, the price of the put option depends on a strike price, and option increases with the strike price. Since the put option makes a profit in the case of prices drop, profits will be higher if the strike price is higher. This is why the bear put spread is a debit range. Specifically, the investor loses the difference between the price at which he buys and sells options. Given that the maximum loss is limited, the worst that can happen is that, at the moment of maturity, the share price is to be above the most of the strike prices. In this case, both of the put options are worthless and the loss is limited to the amount of the premium.

As always, this trade can be reversed to deal with falling prices. It can also be implemented in both directions with both puts and calls. You have to determine the entry point based off the current price and how much you are willing to lose, your expected direction of the stock, and the possible profit, which is capped.

BUTTERFLIES

This one is even more complicated, and it requires three components. The basic idea is to buy one low, in-the-money call, selling two at-the-money calls, and finally buying a high, out-of-the-money call. This is a strategy for when you expect the market to move sideways, for the highest profit is in the middle and you can maintain a profit within a range. As with most of these strategies involving more than one component, the risk and reward are both limited.

The profit is highest when the spot price is equal to the two written calls. You keep the premium for both written (short) calls, but lose the premiums paid on the two purchased (long) calls. The higher long call is going to cost much less than the short call premiums, as it is far out-of-the-money, but the lower long call is going to cost more since it is either in-the-money or at least closer to being so. The risk is capped at the premiums paid for the long calls. If the underlying is below the lower strike or above the higher strike on your longs, you will incur the maximum loss. From that, you can easily see this strategy is for range trading. You can make big spreads, but keep in mind the profits will be based on how far into the money you are. You can make this more complicated, but you must retain symmetry. Notice that the long and short positions have equal numbers of shares at stake and you should keep your expiration dates the same. Otherwise you will either open yourself up to huge risk or diminish your possible profits.

Butterfly spread should be made by using more than two exercise prices so that it contains three different exercise prices of some of the underlying assets at the same time until maturity. The logic of the assembling the butterfly spread is to take one position along the two extreme exercise prices in options, while the opposite position is occupied by the double number of the same options to a medium exercise price. The butterfly spread is possible with buying and selling options. Long butterfly, either with the call or put options, consists of the purchase of an option with a lower and other options with a higher exercise price, and selling two options with an average exercise price. The long butterfly spread represents a neutral strategy as it expects a stable period.

This spread is not directed to increase or to decrease the price of the underlying assets. The investor who chooses a strategy of short butterfly trading expects a significant change in the price, in any direction, regardless of whether it is rising or falling, of the underlying assets. The short butterfly spread is possible to draw up the buying and selling options. If a short butterfly is made up of put options, the trader sells one option with lower and one with the higher exercise price and buys two put options with an average exercise price. Butterfly range can be made in four different ways, which points to its complexity. This includes:

1. The purchase of a call option with the highest and lowest reasonable price and the simultaneous sale of two call options at an average price.

2. The purchase of a put option with the highest and lowest exercise price and the simultaneous sale of two put options with a high price.

3. The purchase of a call option at the lowest exercise price, and selling call options at an average price along with the

purchase of put options at the highest price, and sell put options at an average exercise price

4. The purchase of put options at the lowest exercise price and selling put options at an average price with the purchase of a call option at the highest exercise price and sell call options at an average exercise price.

CONDOR SPREAD

Condor spread consists of two horizontal spreads of conflicting expectations and includes four options on the same underlying assets with the same due date. Four different exercise prices for each option show the complexity of the Condor spread.

CONDOR SPREAD WITH CALL OPTIONS

The similarity of the condor spread with the butterfly spread is inevitable, but the difference is that in the condor spread there are two different medium exercise prices and the butterfly spread has only one. To perform the long condor spread with the call options trader must buy a call option with a range of exercise price, sell a call option with a slightly higher exercise price, sell a call option with an even greater exercise price, and buy a call option with the highest exercise price.

Condor Spread can be also carried out with the put options so that it consists of purchased put options with the lowest and the one with the highest exercise price, as well as with the two sold put options with the medium exercise price. All four options are relating to the same underlying assets and the due date. Short condor consists of selling the put options with the final exercise price and the purchasing an option with medium exercise price

VERTICAL SPREAD

The simultaneous purchase and sale, purchase or sale of options on the same underlying assets, and the same exercise price, but in different maturities, is resulting in the vertical spread. The vertical spread is referred to as the calendar spread due to the use of different maturities. We can distinguish calendar put spread and calendar call spread. These types of neutral strategies can be focused on the growth and drop in asset prices. Combining the different times of maturity in the compiling spread, the investor combines intrinsic value, and a time value, of occupied positions in a particular option. In this way, in a case of the option with less time, the investor is set to its intrinsic value, while with the options with a longer time to maturity; the investor puts in the time value of options as a primary goal.

CALENDAR SPREAD WITH CALL OPTIONS

When compiling this spread investor takes a short position in the option with a shorter time to maturity, and a long position in the option with a longer time to maturity. The investor sells a call option with a shorter time to maturity and buys one call option that has a longer time to maturity. This is a call option on the same underlying assets, with the same strike price. In this way, the short position is making the investor focus on the intrinsic value of the option, and the second position according to the time value focuses him on the call option.

NEUTRAL CALENDAR SPREAD

If prices rise or fall in relation to the strike price, the composer of the vertical spread is faced with the limited loss. The compiler spread can achieve only limited losses. The primary purpose of the assemblers of neutral calendar spread with call options is the closing before maturity of the call option with a shorter time to maturity, and at the same time, expecting price stability in relation to the strike price. Composer of the spread can record profit of share price which may not be equal to the strike price, but which also will not be much further than the strike price of the call option with a shorter time to maturity. The ideal situation is when the share price is somewhat below, or at the level of strike price options. In this way, the shorter option expires worthless and the investor closes the range with a single premium, which increases his profit.

BULLS' CALENDAR SPREAD

These are aggressive calendar spreads that have bull's expectations, therefore, focused on the increase in share prices or other property. Bull's calendar spread is within a certain range also neutral, it is compiled with the current market price that is below the strike price of the calendar spread. The advantages of such spread are lower initial cost and a good chance of making the profit, but with significant risk.

To compiler of the bull calendar spread, achieved profits are required in two events. First, he will make a call option with a shorter time to maturity (short option) which should expire worthlessly. Therefore, the range and draw up options go beyond - because the money is likely to call option with a shorter time to maturity. In this way, the investor is left with a call option with a longer time to maturity (longer optional). Secondly, it is necessary to increase the prices of the underlying assets in the strike price range, after the maturity date of options. If price increases, the investor will make a profit.

CALENDAR SPREAD WITH PUT OPTIONS

Besides with the call options, calendar spread can be put together and with the put options. Similar to the calendar spread with call options, this kind of spread should be made by selling a put option with a shorter time to maturity, and the purchase of put options with longer time of maturity.

Unlike the calendar spread with call options, the calendar spread with put options is a little bit more protected by neutral strategy at the lower limit potential losses. Also, it is a debit spread, regardless of what was sold and purchased, and put options have the same executable price because, in all of this, the only important thing is that the purchased put option has a higher time value.

WRITING COVERED CALL OPTION

This strategy is used by sellers to buy and sell options. In order to protect the seller from the always present, risk position closes the opening positions on the futures market or buying and selling a futures contract that will suit the conditions specified in the option. In this way, the risk is reduced, but at the same time so is the profit potential as well.

THE PREPARATION OF COVERED CALL OPTIONS

The purchase option is considered covered if its compiler sold the call option on the owned underlying assets Therefore, the compiler has bought shares or other underlying assets constituted the purchase option. Purchase options can be used as collateral assets of falling prices so that the loss is mitigated by the premium received from the investor for the sold call option. So writing covered call options can be used as insurance against falling value of the underlying assets.

As an example of covered call options, we can take the trader who owns a futures contract on gold. Current futures price is $ 1,030 / ounce (contract on 100 ounces). The trader has to protect against the risk and decides to sell the contract purchase option for the exercise price $ 1,050 / ounce. For a written option an investor receives a premium of $ 20 / ounce. Writing covered call options will bring better results than long futures positions in following these cases:

• If the forward price of gold, at the end of the options, remains the same, meaning $ 1,030 /   ounce, the trader earns the premium, i.e. $ 20 / ounce. In this case, the buyer who sold the   call option makes more sense to buy gold on the market at $ 1,030 / ounce than with the   executive agreed price that is $ 1,050 / ounce. For this reason, the customer will leave the option to expire.

• If the forward price of gold rises to the exercise price of $ 1,050 / ounce futures contract is now worth $ 105,000.00 (1050 x 100). As in the previous case, the buyer will let the option to expire because he can buy gold on the market with the same price which offers the option. In case the buyer decides to buy the gold with a strike price, the trader will earn the profit of 1070 $/ ounce.

• In case that the forward price of the gold drops to the price of 101 $/ ounce, the long forward position will face with the loss of 20$ / ounce which will be compensated by the premium.

• In case that forward price keeps falling below the 1010$/ ounces, the loss will be, not only with a long forward position but with a covered call as well. It is important to emphasize that loss on the forward and options market are reduced by the amount of received premium.

WRITING THE COVERED PUT OPTION

Writing the covered put option is similar to the strategy of writing the covered call option. This is also a strategy of reduced risk, but at the same time, potential profit is reduced as well. The compiler of the covered put option is selling the put option and a contract with the same date of maturity. The ideal situation for selling the covered put option is in the case when the investor believes that the price of the property will not significantly reduce.

You can find plenty of other strategies online, and if you start trading, you may even discover some independently. The most important takeaways from this section are the risks and rewards are often capped; if you prefer unlimited gains, that is possible

without buying stock and you can enter much more cheaply than actually buying stock. On the other hand, if you are the adrenalin junkie interested in making small profits, writing naked calls might be your paradise. Writing options in itself is not risky. If you have an offsetting position that limits your losses, writing options is a good way to make some extra money on stock you already own or, if you don't own, you could own at a guaranteed price based on another option you already hold. Writing puts may be a good way to make some extra money, especially if you are willing to take more stock at your strike price. Writing naked options is where you can get into a lot of trouble and lose far more than you are prepared to lose. When trading options, there are three main features. The first feature is the possibility of buying/selling or giving up, and the other characteristics are related to the maturity of the options. For each option, the premium has to be paid. Premium ultimately affects the result of the selected strategy. Which strategy will be applied depends on goals of investors, the market knowledge, trading techniques and education. Once the goals, market knowledge, trading techniques and education are considered, it will be easy to decide whether to take simple or most complex options strategy.

It is important to mention the risk of simple strategies. Even though simple strategies give the possibility of higher returns they can also bring larger losses. This is not the case with call option where the customer knows in advance what it is the maximum loss; therefore, it is limited to the amount of premium paid. In contrast to the simple, complex strategies provide unlimited profits with limited risk of failing. They contain several actions, or more investment activities, and require entry into the position with at least two options.

USING OPTIONS FOR INSURANCE

All of the above strategies were illustrated as profit-generating strategies. You can use a lot of them as insurance, too. The most common are to buy put options on a stock you hold that may fall or buy call options on a stock you are eyeing. The former can be used to sell assets you already own if the price takes an unexpected dip. The latter can be used as a sort of "opportunity insurance", where you expect the stock to rise, but you may not be confident enough to lay out thousands of dollars. No worries – just buy some option contracts and if it goes your way, you can still purchase the stock. Of course, there is the possibility of it not going your way and not having done anything would net zero, while buying the options will net you a negative profit (that means a loss).

This strategy also works if you are short equity (keep in mind shorting stock requires a small interest fee paid to the broker, as you are technically borrowing shares). If you are short, you may want to limit your risk by buying call options for a strike above your entry. If you buy it OTM, it will be relatively cheap (since it is a call), but you will be able to cap your losses on the short sale at the premium paid plus the difference between the strike and your short entry price. As a quick example for illustration: if you went into a stock short at $45 and the current spot is $43, you have a small profit. You may expect it to fall further, so you want to stay in the short position, but to limit your risk, you buy a call option at $47. Notice this call is OTM, so it should be relatively cheap. Now, if the price skyrockets to $70, you won't be stuck with a short-selling loss of $70-$45 (which is likely to be a real loss, as brokers will issue a margin call on you), but you will be able to buy shares at $47 to give back to your broker. You lost $2 on the difference plus the premium, but it certainly is better than losing the $35/share.

Some of the other strategies listed above can also be used as insurance. If you hold a stock and expect it to stay in a range, you can set up a trade such that if the stock falls outside the range, you can still limit your losses. You also can create strategies in options to hedge against other open trades in options. For example, if you wrote a naked call, you can write a naked put to offset it. Whether this is one trade strategy or insurance is up to semantics.

CHAPTER FIVE

OPTIONS ON OTHER INSTRUMENTS

While equity options are by far the most common, there are other options and instruments that are also widely used. Futures are more like European options than American because they require delivery of the underlying at the expiration date. There is no option to exercise or not (unless you consider selling the future back to the market as the option). Options can also be purchased on futures, and futures on options, because the financial world is full of innovation. Some of these may be custom only, though, so it may not be something heavily traded or easily found. Further, strategies can involve both futures and options on equities or anything else, since complexity can be used to reduce risk or increase profit.

Futures are used between companies and suppliers, but you can also profit from them. Forex is also used between companies and within companies, but if you have high leverage, forex is also an avenue for you. Options on forex exist, and you can use the same strategies here for forex and futures as you would on equity.

Fixed income, otherwise known as bonds, is also a market for options. Fixed income is much more steady than its potentially volatile futures, forex, and equity markets, so you may not be able to generate as much profit here as in the other markets, but it is still a market to look at if you have experience in FI or have an interest in it.

Keep in mind that equity is highly liquid and does not take a lot of capital to get started in, and as such, equity is probably the best place for a new options trader to start. Whether it be binary, index, single stock, ETF, private stock, or any other equity style, you can use the above strategies to profit or insure. That does not discount the fact, though, that one may use the above strategies and the myriad others found online to trade the other types of financial instruments. Large institutions have customized options on arcane instruments like collateralized debt obligations and credit default swaps. As an individual, it is highly unlikely you will be dealing with these. However, if you are a student or otherwise interested in the financial world, you may want to read up more on this or even pursue this as your future career path.

CONCLUSION

Options can be used to generate profit or as insurance. The insurance fee is generally considered the premium paid. Premiums are based off time to expiration, volatility, and the difference between the spot and strike prices, also known as the intrinsic value. OTM are the cheapest, ATM are the in the middle, and ITM are the most expensive. This is due to intrinsic value. There are two styles of options, American and European, that have different rules governing when one can exercise them. There are two types of options, calls and puts, and they can be mixed for various strategies.

Everything in this book can be used or modified. The most basic strategies are widely applied, and you, as the investor, should modify them to fit your trading strategies and techniques. If you like a lot of risk and are willing to take it for small profits, you may be interested in writing options. If you just want to have a little insurance, go with simple hedging strategies. If you want to speculate, options are a good way to do it without losing a lot of money. You can also leverage yourself, because you can buy the right to 10,000 shares but only pay the premium – you don't have to outlay cash for all 10,000 shares. Even when you execute, you can borrow from your broker since you will turn around and sell the shares straight back to the market.

Options are tightly connected to stocks, but you can have options for futures, forex, or any other financial instrument. If you are a beginning, start out with equity options. If you already trade forex or futures, you can start with those. Either way, options are a good way to make money while simultaneously limiting risk.

Options, like the financial world, can be incredibly innovative and there is nothing stopping you from searching for the most complex, uncommon, arcane options trades out there. But for most of you, happy equity options trading, and I hope you can make some money.

GLOSSARY/REFERENCE

Option: a legal contract to buy or sell an underlying asset at a specific price before a specific date

European-style: option that can only be exercised on expiry date

American-style: option that can be exercised at any time before and on the expiry date

Strike price: the price designated in the option as the agreed buy/sell price

Spot price: the price of the underlying

Put option: an option that provides the holder the right to sell the underlying at the strike price

Call option: an option that provides the holder the right to buy the underlying at the strike price

At-the-money (ATM): An option whose strike price is equal to the spot price

In-the-money (ITM): An option whose strike price is lower/higher than the spot for calls/puts

Out-of-the-money (OTM): an option whose strike price is higher/lower than the spot for calls/puts

Premium: the fee paid for the privilege of purchasing the option; it is made up of time, volatility, and intrinsic values

Long: a position from the holder's perspective that implies they own the instrument

Short: a position from the holder's perspective that implies they do not own the instrument (the holder borrowed or sold the instrument but remains connected through a legal obligation to deliver in the future)

Free Bonus: Join Our Book Club and Receive Free Gifts Instantly

Click Below For Your Bonus:
https://success321.leadpages.co/freebo dymindsoul/

www.ingramcontent.com/pod-product-compliance
Lightning Source LLC
Chambersburg PA
CBHW070039210526
45170CB00012B/538